To

Merry Christmas

Love,

Memories of the Present

A Collection
of Holiday Recipes, Crafts, Customs,
and Helpful Miscellany.

Produced by Jacobs, Visconsi & Jacobs Co.
Cleveland, Ohio USA

Editor
William N. Fullington

Contributing Writers
Edward C. Camp
Sheryl A. Hibler
Gregg A. McCort
John H. McLendon

Illustrator
Debbie Palen

Graphic Design
Carol J. Hunt

·⚬ (CONTENTS) ⚬·

1889

·ᚙ⟨A SHORT HISTORY OF MR. CLAUS⟩ᚙ·

Sinterklass

St. Nicholas

Christkind

Santa Claus

Father Christmas

Kris Kringle

GOOD BOYS & GIRLS

St.

Nicholas; Sinterklass; Christkind; Kriss Kringle; Father Christmas. The names have varied down through the centuries, each one peculiar to the culture which gave birth to its legend. Yet one common thread remains: The idea of an all-knowing, charitable gift giver who makes his appearance on or around Christmas-time, rewarding good little children with presents. We know him as Santa Claus, and his mythic origins can be traced back to the fourth century and a town on the northern shore of the Mediterranean Sea called Myra.

It was in Myra that the legend grew of a young man named Nicholas. A charitable and religious boy, he was said to perform miracles that saved ships from violent storms and provided food for his starving people. Of particular note were his gifts of gold to three unmarried girls whose poverty-stricken father could not afford the dowries that would enable them to marry. It was here that one Christmas tradition was born as one of the bags of gold thrown into the girls' house by Nicholas came to rest in a hanging stocking. Nicholas' reputation as a patron of unmarried girls was eclipsed only by his patronage of children when, as Bishop of Myra, he was said to bring three boys back to life after the lads were killed by an evil innkeeper. These two stories did much to enhance the legend of Nicholas who was made a saint by the Catholic Church after his death in 343 A.D.

St. Nicholas was given the feast day of December 6 and throughout Europe the custom of a figure dressed in red and white vestments who visited small children was born. It was St. Nicholas who rewarded good children; a monster-like companion known by various names punished kids who were not so good.

It was the Dutch who brought St. Nicholas to America in the 17th century under the name of Sint Nicholaas or Sinterklaas. They named their first church after him in the city they called New Amsterdam (later, New York City). Soon after, the English gained control of the city and while they accepted the legend of St. Nicholas, they saw fit to translate his Dutch name of Sinterklaas to something a little more Anglican — Santa Claus.

The German settlers who came to America and their Swiss counterparts had their own ideas of a kindly giftgiver. Having rejected St. Nicholas after the Protestant reformation, they created a childlike figure known as the Christkind or Christ child. Children would leave nuts and cookies for this gift giver who would eventually take on the more familiar name of Kriss Kringle. As various cultures came into contact with one another throughout the 1700's, Kriss Kringle took on so many of Santa Claus' characteristics, it was difficult to tell the difference between the two.

(St. Nicholas)

(Christkind)

The image we have of Santa Claus today can be traced to two sources: Dr. Clement Clarke Moore and Thomas Nast. It was Moore who, on the night of December 23, 1822, read to his children a poem he had composed entitled "A Visit From St. Nicholas." Published by a local newspaper shortly thereafter, Moore's prose created a sensation. Here was the legend of St. Nicholas brought to life with sleighs and reindeer, stockings and chimneys, bags of toys, and most of all, a jolly old elf, bearded white and dressed in fur. Moore had taken a figure bound by religious history and native custom and added heaping helpings of fantasy and wonder. Santa Claus would never be the same again.

Thomas Nast drew on Moore's interpretation and forever defined Santa Claus in illustration. A political cartoonist during the Civil War, Nast wanted to create a happier world than the real one he was depicting. His first drawing of Santa however, was a compromise. Captioned "Santa in Camp", it showed Santa dressed in stars and stripes giving toys to the troops. In subsequent drawings, Nast would refine his Santa, making the eyes more expressive, the belly rounder, the beard fuller. Nast gave birth to a more genteel, grandfatherly Santa with an ever-present pipe and jolly smile, a friend to children everywhere. If he had never drawn Santa Claus, Thomas Nast would have gone down in history as a great political cartoonist. Instead, his concept of Santa Claus, a concept that holds true today, stands as his greatest achievement.

Nast's Santa Claus would be interpreted by many artists well into the 20th century. The definite enhancement came at the hand of artist Haddon Sundblom who, through the use of color and shading techniques, produced an even warmer and more expressive Santa. Yet by 1889, the classic image we hold today of Santa Claus had been defined. Variations continue to be made but the Santa Claus born of ancient legend and brought to life through the works of Moore and Nast is the image that endures.

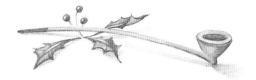

1901

ᴄ(CHRISTMAS CAROLS MADE IN AMERICA)ᴏ

As Americans celebrated the holidays in the century's second year, they sang more and more carols composed by American writers. Traditionally, most Christmas songs originated in Europe and were brought to these shores by seafaring travelers. Beginning in the mid-1800's, American composers began using their talents to create American Christmas songs. By the turn of the century, carols such as "We Three Kings of Orient Are" and "Away in a Manger" had become American Christmas standards.

We Three Kings of Orient Are

John H. Hopkins, Jr. (1820-1891)

John H. Hopkins, Jr.

We three kings of O-ri-ent are; Bearing gifts we traverse a-far,
Born a King on Bethle-hem's plain, Gold I bring to crown Him a-gain,

Field and fountain, moor and mountain, Following yon-der star.
King for ev-er, ceas-ing nev-er, O-ver us all to reign.

O star of won-der, star of night, Star with roy-al beau-ty bright,

Westward leading, still pro-ceed-ing, Guide us to Thy per-fect light.

O Little Town of Bethlehem

Phillips Brooks (1835-1893)

Lewis H. Redner (1831-1908)

O lit-tle town of Bethle-hem, How still we see thee lie!
For Christ is born of Ma-ry, And gathered all a-bove,

A-bove thy deep and dreamless sleep The si-lent stars go by;
While mortals sleep, the an-gels keep Their watch of wond'ring love.

Yet in thy dark streets shin-eth The ev-er-last-ing Light;
O morning stars, to-geth-er Pro-claim the ho-ly birth,

The hopes and fears of all the years Are met in thee to-night.
And prais-es sing to God the King, And peace to men on earth!

Away in a Manger

William James Kirkland (1847?-?)   William James Kirkland

A- way in a manger, no crib for His bed, The lit- tle Lord
The cat- tle are lowing, the Ba- by a-wakes, But lit- tle Lord

Je- sus laid down His sweet head. The stars in the sky looked
Je- sus, no cry- ing He makes. I love Thee, Lord Je- sus; look

down where He lay, The lit- tle Lord Je- sus, a- sleep on the hay.
down from the sky, And stay by my cradle till morning is nigh.

1911

WHEN CHRISTMAS TREES MADE THEIR OWN LIGHT.

Before electric tree lights and before store~bought ornaments, families usually made their own tree decorations. Using natural materials found in the countryside or simple household odds and ends, a creative eye and nimble fingers often produced works of art now rarely seen. It's not surprising to see the same practice~ and ideas~ being revived today.

POPCORN and CRANBERRY
·GARLANDS·

Here's a way to create garland using simple household items:

popcorn (day-old works best)
cranberries (try freezing fresh ones before threading them)
thread
a needle
and
a few shirt buttons

Thread a needle with about 5 feet of strong thread, tying a big knot on the end. Then take a shirt button and thread it on the needle. Now start creating your garland by alternating popcorn and cranberries on the strand.

When you have filled the strand, take off the needle and thread another button on the end of the string. Leave enough string to tie two strands together as needed.

Another Tip:
Create extra strands of garland and use them to feed the birds outside. Simply take the strands and use them to decorate the trees in your yard. Think of it as a little Christmas present to the wildlife. And after Christmas, don't throw away the garland. Take it and place on the trees for the birds to enjoy.

APPLE and CLOVE
·SACHET BALLS·

Fill your house with the extraordinary fragrance of Christmas by using some very ordinary items:

apples   **decorative ribbon**
whole cloves   **needle & thread**

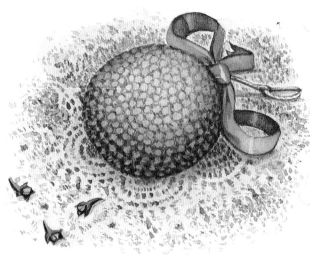

Take an average-size apple and prepare it for hanging by using a long needle, black thread and a button. Thread the button with the needle and run it through the apple, starting at the bottom and coming out the top. Pull the button flush with the bottom of the apple, then tie the thread in a loop large enough to serve as an ornament hanger.

Next, take cloves and insert them three-fourths of the way into the apple. Completely fill the apple's surface with cloves so that the shape is all that is visible. We suggest placing the apples on cheese cloth or wax paper to absorb any juices that escape. Over time, the cloves preserve the apple, making it shrink somewhat.

FROSTED PINE CONE

Use a little imagination to convert those pine cones in your backyard into beautiful tree ornaments by using:

white glue
salt
floral wire
small pine cones

First, take the salt and pour it into a small bowl. "Frost" the pine cones with white glue by placing small amounts on the pine cone "petals."

Before the glue dries, roll the pine cone in the salt to create a lasting frosting effect. Allow the pine cone to dry, then create an ornament hanger by using floral wire. Insert the wire in the bottom of the pine cone, wrapping it around the stem several times for good measure. (For a different effect, try grouping the pine cones using the hanger to connect them.)

You might try using the ornament as a special decoration in your handmade wreaths, table centerpieces or garland decorations.

MODELED ORNAMENTS

Create modeling clay using simple household staples. You will need:

1 cup of regular wheat flour
(non-self rising)
1/2 cup salt
1 teaspoon of powdered alum
1/2 cup water (add small amount of food coloring if desired)

Combine all dry ingredients in a bowl and slowly add water a little at a time, mixing until reaching the consistency of pie dough. Knead the mixture to a smooth consistency.

Use your mixture as you would modeling clay, creating different shapes and designs. A favorite design with children are ornaments having their names "engraved" on them. Or, flatten out and cut with cookie cutters to create different shapes. The clay dries in about three days, or can be baked at very low heat for a few hours until dry. Before you allow your designs to dry, poke a small hole in the top to accommodate string for hanging the ornament.

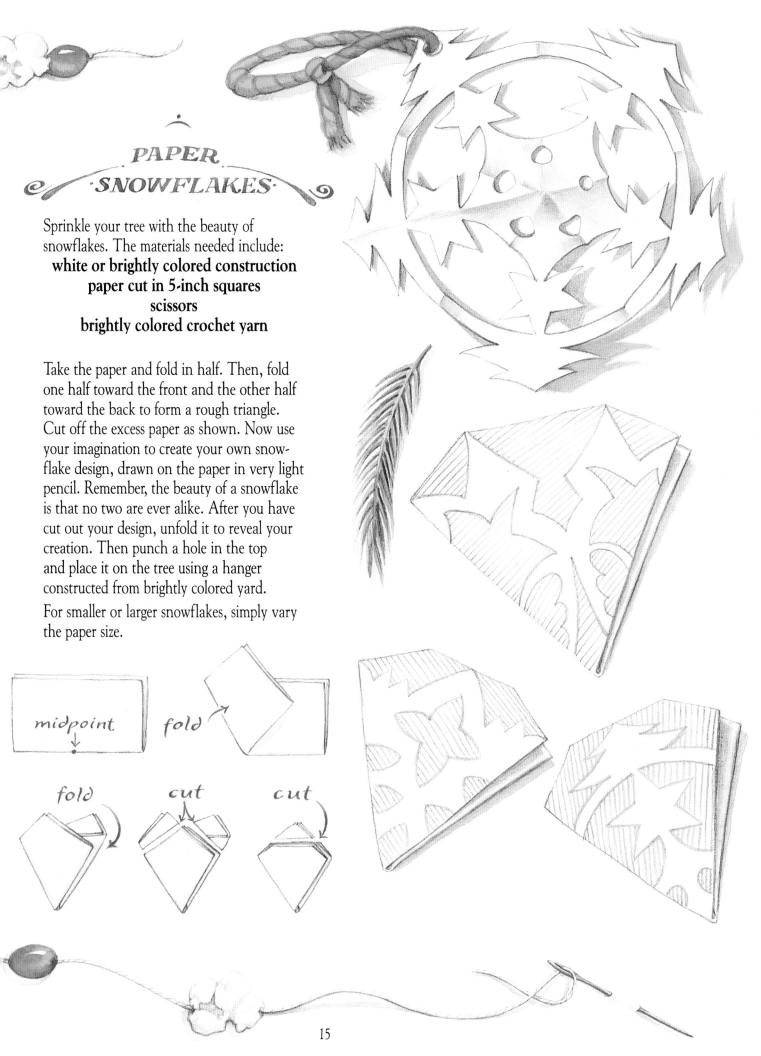

PAPER SNOWFLAKES

Sprinkle your tree with the beauty of snowflakes. The materials needed include:

white or brightly colored construction paper cut in 5-inch squares
scissors
brightly colored crochet yarn

Take the paper and fold in half. Then, fold one half toward the front and the other half toward the back to form a rough triangle. Cut off the excess paper as shown. Now use your imagination to create your own snowflake design, drawn on the paper in very light pencil. Remember, the beauty of a snowflake is that no two are ever alike. After you have cut out your design, unfold it to reveal your creation. Then punch a hole in the top and place it on the tree using a hanger constructed from brightly colored yard.

For smaller or larger snowflakes, simply vary the paper size.

midpoint   *fold*

fold   *cut*   *cut*

BROOMSTRAW ·STARS·

Fill your tree with stars made from old-fashioned brooms. Here's what you'll need to make them:

one standard-size broom with real broom straws
brightly colored embroidery thread or crochet yarn
white glue

Each star is constructed of five broom straw bundles. Make the bundles by clipping about a dozen broom straws at least six inches in length from the broom. Gather them in bundles and place white glue about an inch from both ends. Then take the thread and wrap it tightly around the bundles, over the glue, at least three times. Tie both ends and then let them dry. Clip the straws to even up the ends.

Next, take the bundles and form a star. Everywhere the bundles touch one another, gently lift up and place a spot of glue. After all have been glued, place a heavy book on top of the star and let it dry. Take the brightly colored thread and make a loop to use in hanging the star. You can even take the thread and tie a single knot at each point where the bundles touch.

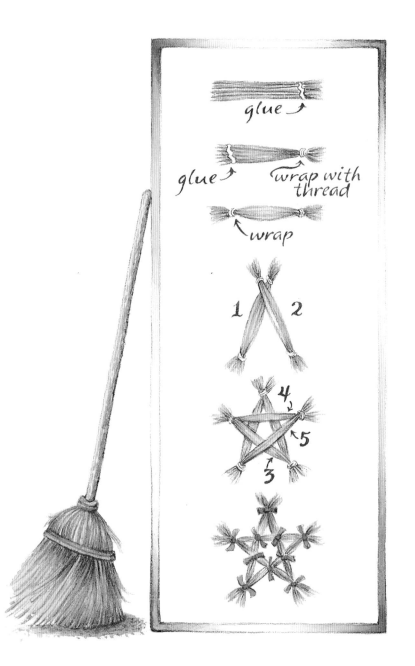

COOKIE ORNAMENTS

Use your favorite cookie shapes to create a beautifully simple decoration. Start by stirring up your favorite cookie mixture that produces a pretty sturdy cookie dough. (We suggest a sugar cookie mixture.) Use a drinking straw to poke a hole in the top of the cookie before you bake it. Bake the cookies, decorate and let them cool. Then take brightly colored ribbon or crochet thread, thread it through the hole and hang on the tree. For fun, be sure to make all sorts of shapes and sizes and decorate with family names. (And don't forget to bake enough extras to enjoy while you're decorating the tree.)

CINNAMON STICK ORNAMENTS

Fill your house with the smells of Christmas by making tree ornaments from cinnamon sticks. You need:

whole cinnamon sticks cut in 3-4 inch lengths
bright red ribbon about 1/4 inch wide
white glue

Take three cinnamon sticks and arrange in a small bundle, stacking the sticks in a pyramid shape. Then, place white glue at the points where the cinnamon sticks touch. Allow the glue to dry. To hang on the tree, take brightly colored ribbon and tie a single knot around the middle of the bundle, then place a dab of glue underneath the ribbon and allow it to dry. Be sure to leave enough ribbon to create a loop for hanging. For added fragrance, glue several whole cloves to the cinnamon sticks.

In the years before television, families spent their evenings entertaining themselves with stories or songs. Here's a poem they shared at Christmas that's just as spellbinding today.

A VISIT FROM ST. NICHOLAS

CLEMENT CLARKE MOORE

Twas the night before Christmas, when all through the house
Not a creature was stirring, not even a mouse.
The stockings were hung by the chimney with care,
In hopes that St. Nicholas soon would be there.
The children were nestled all snug in their beds,
While visions of sugar-plums danced in their heads;
And mamma in her kerchief, and I in my cap,
Had just settled our brains for a long winter's nap —
When out on the lawn there arose such a clatter
I sprang from my bed to see what was the matter.
Away to the window I flew like a flash,
Tore open the shutter, and threw up the sash.
The moon on the breast of the new-fallen snow
Gave a lustre of midday to objects below;
When what to my wondering eye should appear
But a miniature sleigh and eight tiny reindeer,
With a little old driver, so lively and quick,
I knew in a moment it must be St. Nick!
More rapid than eagles his coursers they came,
And he whistled and shouted and called them by name,
"Now, Dasher! now, Dancer! now, Prancer and Vixen!
On, Comet! on, Cupid! on, Donder and Blitzen! —
To the top of the porch, to the top of the wall,
Now, dash away, dash away, dash away all!"

As dry leaves that before the wild hurricane fly,
When they meet with an obstacle mount to the sky,
So, up to the housetop the coursers they flew,
With a sleigh full of toys — and St. Nicholas, too.
And then, in a twinkling, I heard on the roof
The prancing and pawing of each little hoof.
As I drew in my head and was turning around,
Down the chimney St. Nicholas came with a bound:
He was dressed all in fur from his head to his foot,
And his clothes were all tarnished with ashes and soot;
A bundle of toys he had flung on his back,
And he looked like a peddler just opening his pack.
His eyes, how they twinkled! his dimples, how merry!
His cheeks were like roses, his nose like a cherry;
His droll little mouth was drawn up like a bow,
And the beard on his chin was as white as the snow.
The stump of a pipe he held tight in his teeth,
And the smoke, it encircled his head like a wreath.
He had a broad face and a little round belly
That shook, when he laughed, like a bowl full of jelly.
He was chubby and plump — a right jolly old elf:
And I laughed when I saw him, in spite of myself;
A wink of his eye, and a twist of his head,
Soon gave me to know I had nothing to dread.
He spoke not a word, but went straight to work,
And filled all the stockings; then turned with a jerk,
And laying his finger aside of his nose,
And giving a nod, up the chimney he rose.
He sprang to his sleigh, to his team gave a whistle,
And away they all flew like the down of a thistle.
But I heard him exclaim, ere they drove out of sight,

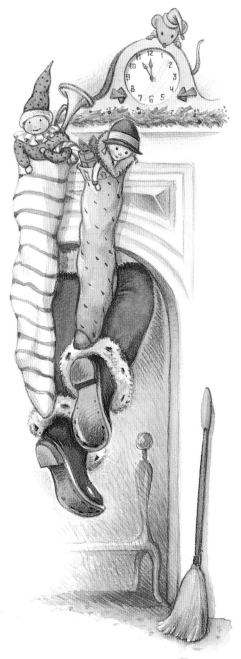

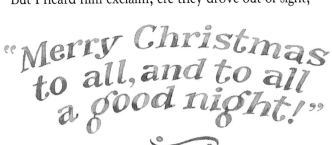

"Merry Christmas
to all, and to all
a good night!"

1944

·◦ (DELICIOUS CHRISTMAS FARE) ◦·

All across America, Christmas combines the best of long-standing traditions and new ideas. As Americans, we are blessed with customs handed down from cultures all over the world. When combined with Yankee ingenuity, the results are, in a word, delicious.

·BASIC BREAD STUFFING & VARIATIONS·

1 cup butter or margarine
4 cups chopped celery
1 cup chopped onion
4 quarts soft bread cubes
1 tablespoon salt
1½ teaspoons poultry seasoning
½ teaspoon rubbed sage
½ teaspoon pepper
hot broth or water

Melt butter in large skillet; add celery and onion and cook until tender but not brown. Stir occasionally. Combine with bread cubes, salt, poultry seasoning, sage and pepper.

Mix lightly. Add enough broth to moisten.

Yield: Approximately 4 quarts, enough for 14 - 18-pound turkey.

Giblet Stuffing: Add chopped, cooked giblets. Use giblet broth as liquid.

Apple Stuffing: Add 1 cup pared, chopped apple to celery and onion; cook until tender, 3 - 5 minutes.

Chestnut Stuffing: Add 4 cups boiled, chopped chestnuts. Substitute milk for broth or water.

Mushroom Stuffing: Cook 1/2 pound mushrooms, sliced, with celery and onion.

·OPEN PAN ROAST TURKEY·

After stuffing the turkey, truss it and rub the breast with some butter. Sprinkle with flour, salt and pepper. Place the turkey on a rack in a shallow pan with breast side up. Loosely cover with foil and place in a hot oven at 325° and cook according to the following chart.

Baste often and remove foil approximately 20 minutes prior to the end of cooking time.

When the turkey is done, put it on a warm serving dish and keep it warm in a low oven while you make the gravy.

COOKING CHART

6-8 lbs.	3½-4 hrs.
8-12 lbs.	4-4½ hrs.
12-16 lbs.	4½-5½ hrs.
16-20 lbs.	5½-6½ hrs.
20-24 lbs.	6½-7½ hrs.

· TURKEY GRAVY ·

Rinse giblets, with the exception of the liver, and place them in a small saucepan with an onion, carrot, salt, pepper and bouquet garni, (or use a combination of spices, such as parsley, sage, thyme, etc.) Cover with water and simmer slowly. When the meat has cooked, discard giblets, onion, carrot and bouquet garni. Set broth aside. Remove cooked turkey and place on a serving dish. Pour off as much fat as possible from the roasting pan. Add a glass of white wine (optional) to the remaining juices and cook over a medium heat, scraping any sediment from the bottom. Mix 3 teaspoons of softened butter with 3 teaspoons of flour and add this gradually to the pan. Add the giblet broth. Stir well and cook until sauce is glossy and slightly thickened. Keep covered until required and serve in a hot sauce boat.

·CRUNCHY SWEET POTATOES·

4 sweet potatoes or yams, cooked, drained and peeled
¼ cup butter or margarine
¼ cup packed brown sugar
½ teaspoon salt
Dash ground cinnamon
⅓ cup light cream or milk

Topping:
⅓ cup light brown sugar
2 cups of cornflakes
1 cup chopped pecans
½ cup melted butter

Mash potatoes; stir in butter, brown sugar, salt and cinnamon. Add cream, beating till fluffy. Turn into a shallow 1½-quart casserole. In a separate bowl, combine topping ingredients. Sprinkle topping evenly and bake in a 325° oven for 30 minutes or until topping is brown.

Makes 8 servings.

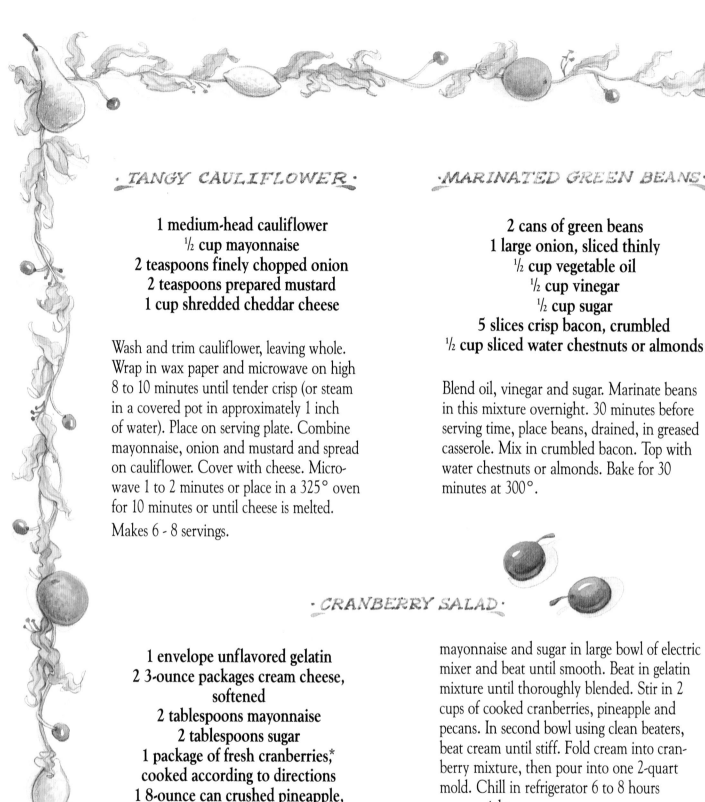

· TANGY CAULIFLOWER ·

1 medium-head cauliflower
½ cup mayonnaise
2 teaspoons finely chopped onion
2 teaspoons prepared mustard
1 cup shredded cheddar cheese

Wash and trim cauliflower, leaving whole. Wrap in wax paper and microwave on high 8 to 10 minutes until tender crisp (or steam in a covered pot in approximately 1 inch of water). Place on serving plate. Combine mayonnaise, onion and mustard and spread on cauliflower. Cover with cheese. Microwave 1 to 2 minutes or place in a 325° oven for 10 minutes or until cheese is melted.

Makes 6 - 8 servings.

· MARINATED GREEN BEANS ·

2 cans of green beans
1 large onion, sliced thinly
½ cup vegetable oil
½ cup vinegar
½ cup sugar
5 slices crisp bacon, crumbled
½ cup sliced water chestnuts or almonds

Blend oil, vinegar and sugar. Marinate beans in this mixture overnight. 30 minutes before serving time, place beans, drained, in greased casserole. Mix in crumbled bacon. Top with water chestnuts or almonds. Bake for 30 minutes at 300°.

· CRANBERRY SALAD ·

1 envelope unflavored gelatin
2 3-ounce packages cream cheese, softened
2 tablespoons mayonnaise
2 tablespoons sugar
1 package of fresh cranberries,*
cooked according to directions
1 8-ounce can crushed pineapple, drained
½ cup chopped pecans
1 cup heavy cream
Lettuce leaves

Sprinkle gelatin over ¼ cup cold water in small bowl and let stand 5 minutes to soften. Add ¼ cup boiling water, stirring to dissolve. Set aside to cool. Combine cream cheese,

mayonnaise and sugar in large bowl of electric mixer and beat until smooth. Beat in gelatin mixture until thoroughly blended. Stir in 2 cups of cooked cranberries, pineapple and pecans. In second bowl using clean beaters, beat cream until stiff. Fold cream into cranberry mixture, then pour into one 2-quart mold. Chill in refrigerator 6 to 8 hours or overnight.

To serve: Dip mold briefly in bowl of hot water, then insert tip of knife between edge of mold and salad to loosen. Invert salad onto a serving plate and surround with lettuce leaves and garnish with remaining cranberries.

Makes 8 servings.

*May substitute with 1 16-ounce can of whole cranberry sauce.

·MUFFINS·

3 cups all-purpose flour
1 teaspoon salt
$\frac{1}{3}$ oz. fresh yeast
1 teaspoon granulated sugar
1-$1\frac{1}{4}$ cups warm milk
1 egg, beaten
2 tablespoons butter, melted

Sift the flour and salt into a large bowl. Cream the yeast and sugar with three tablespoons of the warm milk and let it stand in a warm place until it is frothy. Stir the yeast mixture into the flour together with the beaten egg and the melted butter and enough of the warm milk to make a soft dough. Turn the dough on to a floured board and knead until soft and elastic. Place the dough in a large greased plastic bag covered with a cloth and put in a warm place for about one hour, until it has doubled in size. Turn the dough back on to the floured board, punch it down and divide it into 16 pieces. Roll out each piece into a circle $2\frac{3}{4}$ in across and $\frac{3}{8}$-$\frac{3}{4}$ thick. Cover the muffins with a piece of greased wrap and allow to rise again for 15-20 minutes. Cook them gently a few at a time on a greased griddle or in a heavy frying pan for just under 10 minutes on each side. When they are cooked keep them warm until they are all ready, pull them apart using two forks, butter them and serve immediately. It is important not to cut them with a knife as this will make them "sad" in the middle. Any muffins not required can be split and toasted the next day.

·BANANA PUMPKIN BREAD·

3 to 4 extra-ripe, medium bananas, peeled
1 cup cooked mashed pumpkin
3 eggs
$1\frac{1}{2}$ cups sugar
1 cup vegetable oil
5 cups all-purpose flour
1 tablespoon baking soda
2 teaspoons ground cinnamon
$\frac{1}{2}$ teaspoon ground cloves
2 cups chopped walnuts

Slice bananas into blender, whir until puréed (2 cups). Combine bananas, pumpkin, eggs and sugar in mixer bowl. Beat in oil. Combine remaining ingredients except walnuts. Beat into banana mixture until just blended. Stir in walnuts. Pour into 3 greased ($8\frac{1}{2}$ x $4\frac{1}{2}$ inch) loaf pans. Bake in 350°F oven 50 to 60 minutes until toothpick inserted comes out clean. Cool in pan 10 minutes. Turn onto wire racks to complete cooling.

Makes 3 loaves.

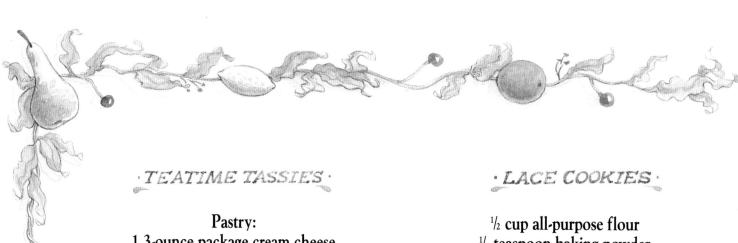

· TEATIME TASSIES ·

Pastry:
1 3-ounce package cream cheese
½ cup butter or margarine
1 cup flour

Blend cream cheese and butter. Mix in flour and chill for one hour. Shape into two dozen balls and place in tiny ungreased muffin cups. Press dough on bottom and sides of cup.

Pecan Filling:
1 egg
¾ cup brown sugar
1 tablespoon soft butter or margarine
1 teaspoon vanilla
Dash of salt
⅔ cup coarsely broken pecans

Beat together everything except pecans. Divide pecans among pastry lined cups. Add egg mixture. Bake in a 325° oven for 25 minutes or until filling is set. Cool and remove from muffin pans.

Makes 2 dozen.

· NUT CRESCENTS ·

1 cup shortening, mostly butter
⅓ cup granulated sugar
⅔ cup nuts — ground
¼ teaspoon salt
1⅔ cup flour

Cream butter and sugar thoroughly. Add rest of ingredients. Form into crescents. Bake in 350° oven for approximately 20 minutes. Sprinkle with powdered sugar while still warm.

· LACE COOKIES ·

½ cup all-purpose flour
¼ teaspoon baking powder
½ cup sugar
6 tablespoons butter, melted
¾ cup oats
2 tablespoons heavy cream
2 tablespoons light corn syrup
1 tablespoon vanilla

Preheat oven to 350.° Sift together flour, baking powder and sugar. Add remaining ingredients and mix well. Drop ¼ teaspoonfuls of the batter 4 inches apart on an ungreased cookie sheet. Bake 8 to 10 minutes or until golden. Let cool before removing.

Makes 4 dozen cookies.

· CHRISTMAS SUGAR COOKIES ·

3 cups sugar
3 sticks butter
3 eggs
4 cups flour

Mix together sugar and butter until smooth. Add eggs, mixing after each. Fold in flour until blended. Dough should be firm but of a manageable consistency. On lightly floured surface, roll the dough out to ¼-in. thickness. Cut the dough with floured cookie cutters into various shapes. Bake at 375° for 5 to 8 minutes, until a light golden brown. Be careful, because they burn easily.

·SPICED NUTS·

1 egg white
1 tablespoon water
3 cups macadamia nuts or walnuts
¼ cup sugar
½ teaspoon salt
1 teaspoon ground cinnamon
¼ teaspoon ground cloves
¼ teaspoon ground nutmeg

Beat egg white and water until foamy; stir in macadamia nuts, coating well. Combine sugar and remaining ingredients; sprinkle over macadamia nuts, and stir until evenly coated. Spread the nuts in a lightly greased jellyroll pan. Bake at 300° for 25 to 30 minutes, stirring every 10 minutes.

Yield: 3 cups.

·CHRISTMAS JELLY CANDY·

5 envelopes unflavored gelatin
½ cup sugar
2 cups desired fruit juice, fruit nectar or fruit drink (such as cranberry, grape, orange or apricot)
2 tablespoons lemon juice

In a medium saucepan combine the unflavored gelatin and sugar. Add the fruit juice, fruit nectar or fruit drink; let stand for 5 minutes. Bring mixture to boiling; reduce heat. Cook and stir till gelatin dissolves. Add lemon juice. Pour into shallow baking pans. Chill till firm, then loosen sides. Carefully turn out of pans, using a wide spatula. Cut with cookie cutters and place on a wire rack to dry. Store cutouts in single layers between waxed paper in airtight containers up to 5 days. Makes 24 (1½-inch) pieces.

·HOLIDAY PUNCH·

½ cup Real Lemon brand juice
1 12 ounce can orange juice
⅔ orange juice can of water
¼ cup maraschino cherry juice
1 quart gingerale
1 quart white champagne or non-alcoholic sparkling white wine

Pour all ingredients into large punch bowl. Add ice cubes (or an ice ring for an extra festive touch).

Ladle into punch cups to serve.

Serves 25

·HOT CIDER·

One (1) gallon cider
2 teaspoons honey
6 cloves
2 cinnamon sticks
½ lemon squeezed

Warm to serve.

1956

(O, CHRISTMAS TREE)

Christmas, without a Christmas tree? Unthinkable! And yet, the ancient German tradition of placing an evergreen tree in the house and filling it with beautiful decorations is fairly new to our country. Germans settling here in the 1800's brought their tradition along, usually choosing a fresh spruce tree for their holiday cheer. By the mid-1950's, more Americans were buying their trees than cutting their own. No matter what type you choose this year, your tree will be an expression of all the season means to you.

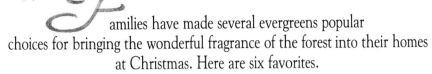

amilies have made several evergreens popular choices for bringing the wonderful fragrance of the forest into their homes at Christmas. Here are six favorites.

Balsam Fir

This tree's fragrance, symmetrical shape, deep green color and ability to retain its needles long after cutting have made this a favorite of many families. The trees range from 25 to 60 feet tall, also making it a favorite for public trees in town squares and parks.

Black Spruce

This slow-growing tree is a favorite for those looking for a small tree. Its needles grow directly from the stout branches, making it a perfect tree for hanging your ornaments.

Scotch Pine

As the tree is not native to the United States, many are grown in tree plantations to be used specifically as Christmas trees. It grows fast and becomes bushy when pruned, making it a favorite for families looking for a fuller tree.

Douglas Fir

These evergreens can grow over 300 feet tall and can live to be over 1,000 years old. Young ones are taken for use as Christmas trees. Its numerous short branches and short, stubby needles offer numerous places for hanging lights and ornaments.

Red Pine

Also known as the Norway pine, this evergreen grows very straight and reaches an acceptable height very quickly. You can recognize it by looking for reddish-brown bark and paired needles growing in groups at the ends of the branches.

Eastern Red Cedar

The very full shape and distinctive fragrance have made this evergreen one of the more recognizable trees. It grows in the wild from the Eastern seaboard to the Plains, so many families who cut their own trees choose this popular evergreen.

·USING EVERY BRANCH·

Almost every family cuts a few branches from the tree in order to get it to fit in the tree stand. Instead of tossing them in the trashcan, use them to create beautiful evergreen sprays. Here's what you'll need:

**2-3 evergreen branches
floral wire
velvet ribbon (1–1/3/4″ Wide),
your choice of color
dried baby's breath of various
stem lengths**

Take the evergreen branches and tie them together at the end with the floral wire. Make several loops around the end to secure the evergreens. Trim any excess with pliers or wire cutters. Next, take the baby's breath and place a longer stem on top of secured ends of the branches, and fill in with shorter pieces. Take floral wire and secure them in place. Take ribbon and wrap around the ends, covering the floral wire. To complete your design, make a simple bow with the ribbon and tie it over the ribbon. Leave plenty of ribbon for streamers. Take scissors and trim the tree branches to create the desired effect. Hang your creation with the ribbon at the top and enjoy the compliments you'll receive.

·MAKE IT SAFE·

Perhaps the most beautiful tree is a safe one. Here are a few simple tips that can mean the difference between a happy Christmas and a needlessly tragic one:

1. Pick a tree from a reliable nursery or retailer that stands behind its products. Carefully inspect the tree before buying it, plucking a test branch to see how easily the needles separate. If they depart with little effort, the tree was probably cut weeks before. Look for locally grown trees if possible.
2. Make sure your tree is watered on a daily basis. At first, you may need to water more than once a day.
3. Locate the tree safely away from heating vents, fireplaces, or any electrical machinery or appliances.
4. Use only UL approved lights and never use lights with frayed wire, loose connections, or lights that burn unreliably. Don't attempt to repair damaged strings of lights — it's better to simply replace them.
5. Beware of overloading any single electrical outlet with too many strings of lights. Don't allow "octopus" outlets to occur. And use only UL approved heavy gauge extension cords that are in like-new condition.
6. Never leave your home with your tree lights still burning. It only takes a few seconds for a dry tree to be totally engulfed in flames.
7. Finally, don't leave your tree standing for extended periods. A maximum of 2-3 weeks is recommended. If your tree is so dry that it is losing large amounts of needles, you should not turn on its lights.

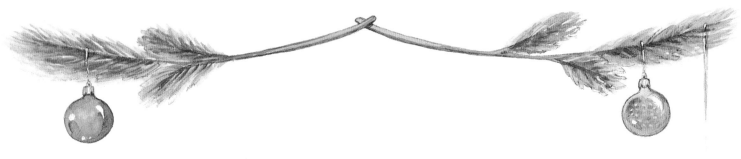

·KEEPING YOUR TREE FRESH·

Nothing fills your house with the smell of Christmas more than a fresh evergreen. To keep your tree fresh, try this formula:

2 tablespoons standard powdered house plant fertilizer (Miracle Grow, etc.)
1 gallon hot water (to aid dissolving)
2 cups light corn syrup
4 tablespoons chlorinated household bleach

Mix the plant food in the hot water, then stir in the corn syrup and bleach. Saw about an inch off the tree trunk. Crush exposed base of the trunk with a hammer. Place the tree in a stand and pour in the solution. Add water daily as it evaporates from the tree stand. (For extra measure, you may want to soak the tree overnight in the solution before placing it in the stand.) Using this recipe, your tree may actually grow!

·LIGHTING THE TREE·

How many lights do you need for your tree? Use the tree's height in determining how many to use. Of course, add as many as you like to get an even fuller effect. This chart offers you a way of deciding how many you'll need to get started.

2 feet	40 bulbs
3 feet	80 bulbs
4 feet	100-120 bulbs
6 feet	200-240 bulbs
7 feet	240-300 bulbs
8 feet	320-360 bulbs

Starting with strings of lights that have end-to-end plugs, place them on your tree by starting at the top and working down. When you have finished, the last plug will be at the bottom and can be easily connected into an outlet or extension cord. Make sure you don't overload your outlet with too many strands; always use heavy gauge extension cords and beware of creating "octopus" outlets.

ENCHANTING GIFTS
&
FESTIVE HOLIDAY TRIMS

The traditions of the holiday season extend from brightly wrapped gifts to festive ornamentation. For many families, adding fresh ideas to those cherished traditions has provided an evolution of holiday decorating and creative expression.

·BABY'S BREATH BOUQUET·

Baby's breath, dried
Narrow velvet ribbon, color of your
choice

Tie small bunches of baby's breath with velvet ribbon. Tie a dainty bow and let ribbon stream from bouquet.

Make as many bouquets as you like and liberally place them all over the tree.

· DECORATIVE ·
· SANTA BOOTS ·

Old snow boots
Red spray paint
White cotton
Glue

Completely spray paint boots and let dry. Glue a cotton band around the top. Fill with candy canes or an arrangement of holly and red berries.

· BURLAP BAG ·
· CANDLE HOLDER ·

Burlap
Plastic bags, bread bags will do
Thread
Sand
Greenery, candles

Sew together as many small burlap bags as you like, approximately the size of a bread bag or slightly bigger and about 12 inches high.

Fill the plastic bags with sand and insert into burlap bag, giving the effect that it is filled.

Fill the top of bags with greenery, apples, and three slender candles.

Use burlap bags singly or in groups. Place on buffet, on hearth, on the mantel, even outside to welcome guests to a party.

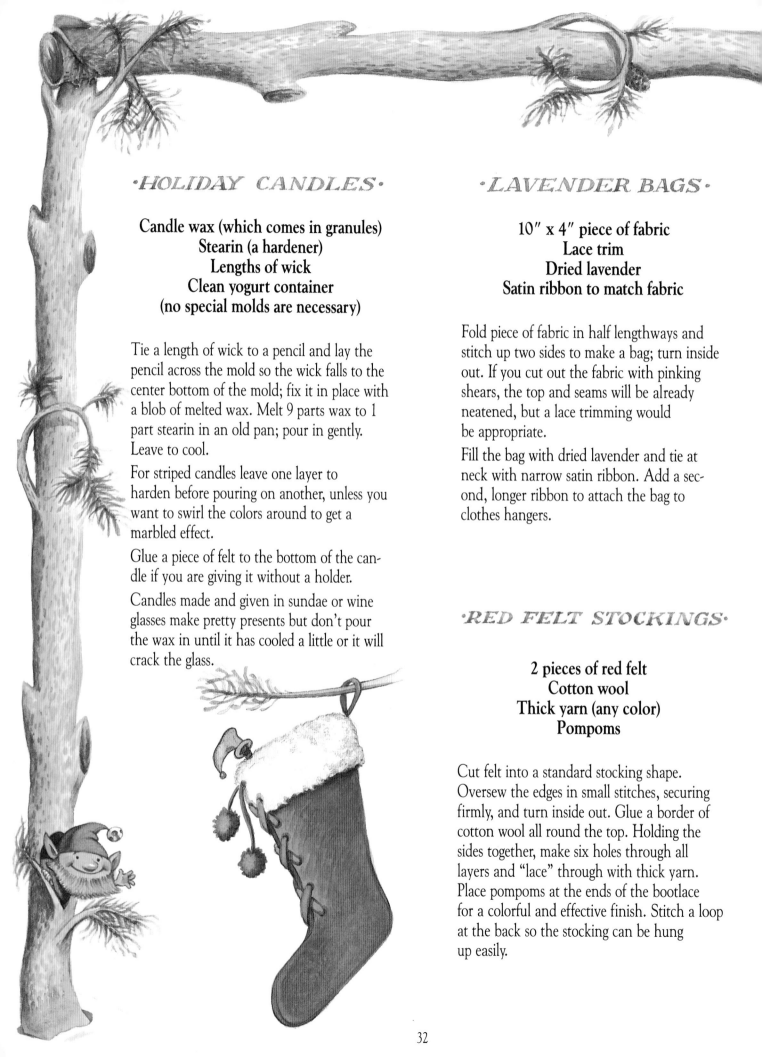

·HOLIDAY CANDLES·

Candle wax (which comes in granules)
Stearin (a hardener)
Lengths of wick
Clean yogurt container
(no special molds are necessary)

Tie a length of wick to a pencil and lay the pencil across the mold so the wick falls to the center bottom of the mold; fix it in place with a blob of melted wax. Melt 9 parts wax to 1 part stearin in an old pan; pour in gently. Leave to cool.

For striped candles leave one layer to harden before pouring on another, unless you want to swirl the colors around to get a marbled effect.

Glue a piece of felt to the bottom of the candle if you are giving it without a holder.

Candles made and given in sundae or wine glasses make pretty presents but don't pour the wax in until it has cooled a little or it will crack the glass.

·LAVENDER BAGS·

10″ x 4″ piece of fabric
Lace trim
Dried lavender
Satin ribbon to match fabric

Fold piece of fabric in half lengthways and stitch up two sides to make a bag; turn inside out. If you cut out the fabric with pinking shears, the top and seams will be already neatened, but a lace trimming would be appropriate.

Fill the bag with dried lavender and tie at neck with narrow satin ribbon. Add a second, longer ribbon to attach the bag to clothes hangers.

·RED FELT STOCKINGS·

2 pieces of red felt
Cotton wool
Thick yarn (any color)
Pompoms

Cut felt into a standard stocking shape. Oversew the edges in small stitches, securing firmly, and turn inside out. Glue a border of cotton wool all round the top. Holding the sides together, make six holes through all layers and "lace" through with thick yarn. Place pompoms at the ends of the bootlace for a colorful and effective finish. Stitch a loop at the back so the stocking can be hung up easily.

PINECONE CANDLE ·HOLDER·

1 large, squat pinecone, 3″ to 5″
in diameter
6 or 8 small pinecones or beechnut
husks, ½″ in diameter
8 or 10 short, full-needle sprigs of
evergreen
1 candle
8″ to 10″ length of florist wire
White glue
Penknife
Silver paint or white flocking (optional)

Loop the florist wire twice around the core of the pinecone near the base. Pull the wire out between the cone's layers so that the ends come out of the bottom. Form a nest around the pinecone by tying the ends of the ever-green sprigs to the wire. Snip off excess wire.

Cut off the top of the pinecone with the pen-knife, making a flat area about two inches in diameter. Glue the smaller cones around the edge, to make a circle large enough to hold your candle. The pinecone can be decorated, if you wish, by frosting its edges with silver paint or white flocking.

Dip melted wax into the center of the pine-cone and mount the candle.

HOLIDAY POTPOURRI ·MIXTURE·

6 Thin-skinned oranges
10 Cinnamon sticks
Cloves
2 ounces Orange oil
6 drops Cinnamon oil

Use a potato peeler to make long strips, about 1/2″ wide, from the oranges. Stud the peels with cloves, about 1/2″-1″ apart. Pour orange oil and cinnamon oil in a bowl and dip peels in oil. Allow excess to drip off rind. Dip cinnamon sticks in mixture as well. Place the potpourri in a glass or ceramic bowl.

Note: Should the scent diminish, reapply oil mixture to peels.

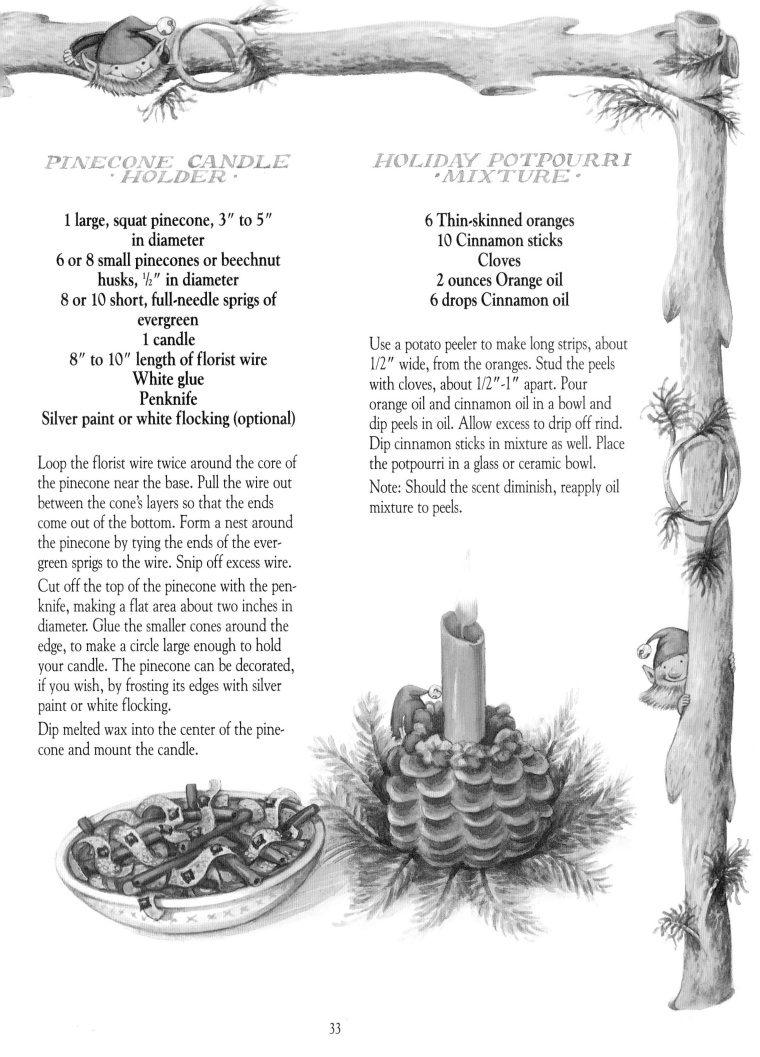

·PINECONE WREATH·

16 inch tier wire wreath frame
Approximately 5-dozen white pinecones
for background
Several large Georgia pine or Norway
spruce cones for focal points. Cones of
different sizes, such as Scotch,
ponderosa, pinon, pitch pine, white
spruce, Douglas fir, hemlock, etc.
Florist wire
Electric glue gun or fast-drying glue
Clear acrylic spray

Place wire wreath rounded side down. Soak white pinecones in water and place them horizontally inside the wire frame with the tip ends in groups of two or three in opposite directions. The wet cones will close, but will partially reopen after drying for several days in a warm place, forming a tight, firm base for the wreath.

When the base is completely dry, wire large cones to the wreath by circling them with wire, pulling the wires to the back, and tying them securely.

Fill in areas with assorted cones, using an electric glue gun to secure them. Trim edges with small cones.

Spray the wreath with clear acrylic and attach a festive holiday ribbon for a decorative accent.

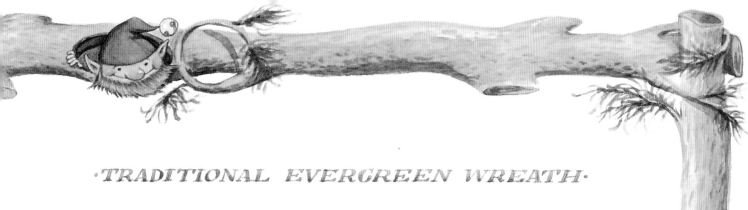

·TRADITIONAL EVERGREEN WREATH·

Wire coat hanger
Large quantity of evergreen sprigs
(24 6″ x 12″ lengths for wreath)
Several spools of florist wire
Pine cones or crab apples
2 yards of wide red ribbon
Wire cutter
Scissors

Constructing the wreath:

Bend the coat hanger so that it forms a circle, leaving the hook on. Wire the ends of two or three bunches of sprigs onto the hanger, near the top. Continue wiring the bunches onto the hanger frame, making sure they lie in the same direction. When the wreath is finished, snip off protruding ends of the wire, and even up the wreath's shape by trimming the greens with scissors.

Make twelve or fifteen small bows and attach them to the wreath with the tail ends of the wire that holds the bow together. You can also attach two or three larger bows instead.

For roping:

Lay out the sprigs so that they overlap, then wire them together. Continue overlapping until desired length is reached.

WRAP IT UP

Surely the most popular tradition of the entire holiday season is that of exchanging gifts. Everyone, young and old alike, enjoys getting nice new things that they've secretly wanted all year. And most important, they also enjoy the good feeling that comes from giving to the ones they care about. Here are some tips that will make your gifts feel even more special.

· HOLIDAY BOWS ·

The traditional finishing touch for holiday
gifts is a pretty bow. They make any package
special and they can also be used with other
holiday decorations. Homemade bows are easy
to make and you can make them any color or
size. The materials you will need for making
them are:

**1-1/2″ ribbon (#9) for each bow
(Use 2″ ribbon for large packages
and wreaths)
23 gauge wire**

The ribbon should be cut into 1-1/2 yard long
strips. The wire should be snipped into 18-
inch lengths. Take a strip of ribbon and hold
it between the thumb and first finger. Wrap
a piece of wire twice around the ribbon, just
above your fingers. Be sure to leave a 3 to
4 inch tail extending from the wire.

Make the first loop behind the wire with the
longer piece of ribbon. The loop should be
about 2-1/2 inches long and pointing up.
Twist the long end of the wire around the
loop and pull it tight.

The second loop should be the same size,
behind the first, but slightly to the side. Continue making loops, with each one pointing
up and cinched tight with a twist of wire at
the center. Each loop should be to one side
of the previous loop. There should be at least
7 loops in each bow.

Cut the excess ribbon and arrange the loops
evenly in a circle. Twist the ends of the wire
together to make a single extension, snip off
the excess, and enjoy your handiwork!

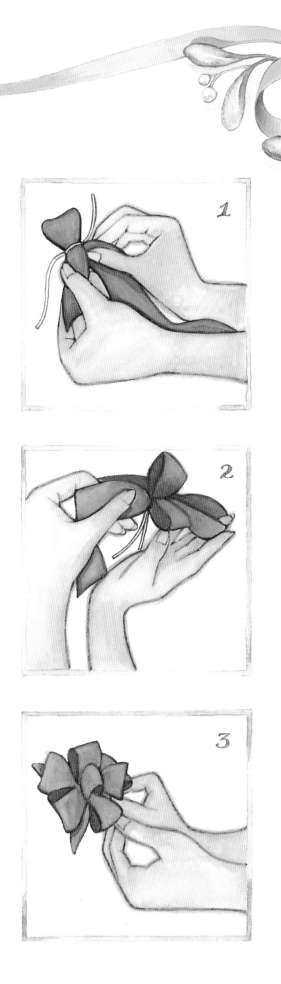

·SIMPLE ORNAMENT BOW·

Many ornaments and decorations call for a very simple bow that becomes a nice detail. Be sure to keep the loops taunt as you knot the center. The center knot should be very tight. This bow is a lot of fun and very easy to make. Just follow these step-by-step instructions.

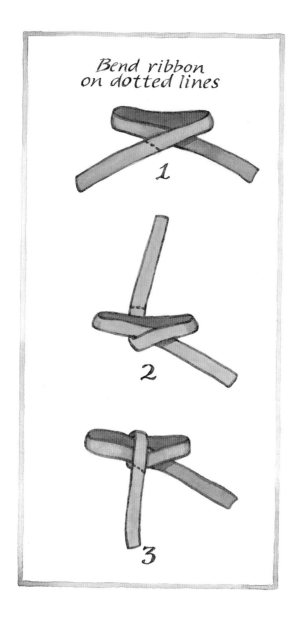

Bend ribbon on dotted lines

1

2

3

4

5

Hold loops taut

& pull ends to tighten knot

6

· IT'S A WRAP ·

Gift wrapping can seem routine and even a chore. But it can be one of the most fun and most creative activities of the holiday season. Here are several suggestions for making a ho-hum chore into a ho-ho presentation.

Making sure the wrapping paper will completely cover the gift can be an awesome task. However, your measurement woes can be solved with a length of string. Simply knot one end of a piece of string and hold it to one side of the gift box and wrap it around the box. Grab it where the string and knot meet. Stretch the string across the paper and add an inch for overlapping. You can use this technique for both the length and the width.

Nothing can spoil a beautiful package more than a messy taping job. Remember that tape should keep lines straight and the paper taunt. Non-reflecting tape or double stick tape are your best choices.

One way to truly personalize a gift is to wrap it in some sort of non-wrapping paper. With a little imagination, you can create a very unique and fresh wrap. Look around your home and you'll find many fun wraps. The following are just a few suggestions:

Use different sections of the newspaper, depending on the person's interests, or use a particular publication, such as The Wall Street Journal for executives. Maps are very interesting because of the various kinds: geographical, nautical, road maps, etc. These are perfect for the frequent traveler. Computer print-out paper, old blueprints and sheet music are all perfect for recognizing particular interests.

Traditional gift-wrapping paper can be spruced up in unconventional ways. It can be decorated by using stencils, image stamps and by attaching items to the package that pertain to the receiver's interests.

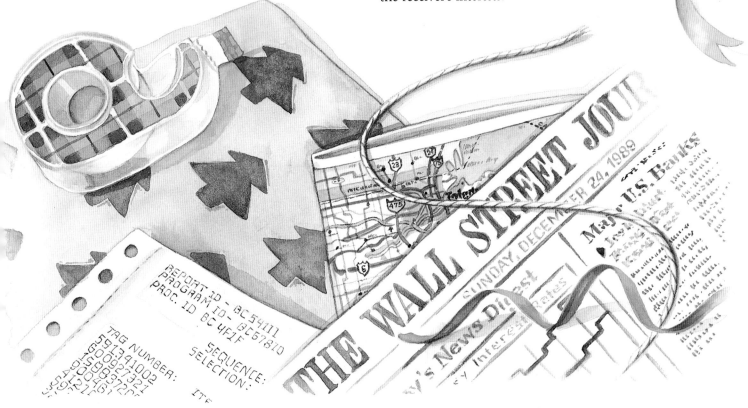

Memories Of The Present

A STORY ABOUT THE BEST GIFT OF ALL

ell me, grandfather," the small boy said. "What did you get for Christmas when you were a little boy?"

"Well, Jason," the old man replied as he held his grandson on his lap, "we didn't have the kinds of toys you have today. Nor did we get as many toys as you probably will this Christmas. But what we received seemed so special and wonderful that I can remember almost every Christmas gift I ever received when I was growing up."

"I can barely remember the presents I got last year," Jason said.

"Well let me tell you a little story about one Christmas when I was not much older than you are now," said the grandfather. "And after you hear it, maybe you'll come to appreciate your gifts so much, you'll always remember them.

When I was a boy, my family lived in a small town where there was only one department store. We didn't have shopping malls in those days. So whenever we needed something, we went to the town square to our little store and bought it.

Those days were almost like magic for me because while my mother and father shopped, I kept hoping we would pass by the toy department so I could catch a glance at all the wonderful things I knew would be there. And every time we went shopping, the last department we'd visit was toys, where I could feast my eyes for what seemed like hours on everything from fire trucks to airplanes to toy trains.

There was one particular December when I walked home from school each day and went out of my way to go through the town square. Because there, in the middle of the front window of Smythe's Department Store was the wagon of my dreams. It was the first metal wagon I'd ever seen and the shine of red paint on it was so bright it seemed to almost glow in the window filled with toys and glistening decorations.

I could stand there with my nose pressed against the glass watching that wagon and never get tired. I made terrific plans for all the ways I could use it. I could run errands to the store for my mother. I could help my father get in wood from the outside. I could go fishing and carry all my fish back in real style. Heck, I could even give rides to little kids and charge them a penny each. Why I'd be rich in no time at all!

I wanted that wagon in the worst way and knew that somehow, if I wished hard enough, I'd get it come Christmas morning. But just to be on the safe side, I wrote a letter to Santa Claus and my dad helped me mail it. And every day on the way home from school, I stopped at Smythe's and watched 'my' wagon until I knew that unless I left, I'd be late for supper. And I sure didn't want to get in trouble so close to Christmas.

Now in those days, people seemed a lot poorer by today's standards. I didn't feel poor, but there weren't too many jobs around then and those who had them didn't make a lot of money. I guess my father was no exception. He was a carpenter by trade and when he was lucky enough to get a job, he'd work from dawn to dusk and I'd hardly ever see him then. I knew there wasn't a lot of money, but still, I hoped Santa would give me that wagon in Smythe's window.

And so, on the last day of school before Christmas, I once again took my usual sidetrip to the town square on my way home to once again stare at that wagon. But when I got there, I saw right away that it was missing.

'Wowee!' I shouted. I just knew that I was going to get it for sure now. The thought never entered my mind that it might have been bought for some other boy or girl. I figured that no other kid wanted that wagon as badly as I. And as devoted as I had been to visiting it every day, it just had to have been bought for me.

I could hardly wait for the few remaining days until Christmas. It seemed like I walked on air with the thought that soon, it would be all mine. I couldn't even concentrate on all the wonderful goodies my mother was making in the kitchen.

Finally it was Christmas Eve night. And even though I felt far too excited to go to sleep, I put on my pajamas early and went to bed without having to be prodded by my parents. Soon, I was sound asleep and dreaming of my big, shiny, red wagon made of metal.

I woke up just as the sun was beginning to rise in the sky. I was instantly wide awake and was so excited, it was all I could do to contain myself as I ran down the steps and into the living room.

As soon as I saw it, my heart sank lower than I think it had ever felt. There was my wagon alright, but it wasn't the one from Smythe's window. This one was made of wood and even though it was painted a bright red, I could tell it hadn't been bought at a store. My name was neatly printed on the side in white paint, but even that didn't lessen the terrible disappointment I felt.

By now, the whole family was up and all I could do was just stand in the middle of the floor and look at the wrong wagon as my brothers and sisters giggled in glee at the presents waiting for them.

I slowly walked over to it and kneeled down beside it. Even though I was badly disappointed, I didn't want to appear ungrateful. I touched the side where my name was printed and noticed there was a note with my name on it sitting inside the wagon. I opened it and began reading.

It said 'Dear Son: Even though you had your heart set on the wagon at Smythe's, it was just too costly for Santa to afford this year. So he made you this very special wagon with his own hands and hopes you like it just as much. Love, Mom and Dad.'

It suddenly struck me that Santa Claus had made me this wagon and had used his time and his talent to make me a gift that could never be bought in a store. I began looking at the wagon with fresh eyes and what I saw made me realize that the best gifts of all are the ones that are given out of love. It didn't really matter anymore to me that the wagon in Smythe's window was under some other kid's Christmas tree. I realized that my wagon was far more special than any other wagon because mine had been made especially for me."

The grandfather had a distant look in his eye as he remembered that Christmas from many years ago. And both he and his grandson knew that the memory of this present was perhaps the best gift either of them had ever received.